Irene Emily Louise Mutton

nee Morris

1920 - 1988

Irene Emily Louise Mutton (nee Morris)
1920 – 1988

Compiled and edited by Peter Bond and Graham Himmelhoch-Mutton

ISBN 978-0-6487713-0-2

First published in Australia in 2020

Peter James Bond, Publisher
ABN 90 679 300 973

COPYRIGHT NOTICE
All rights reserved. No part of this publication may be reproduced, stored in a retrieval system, or transmitted, in any form or by any means, electronic, mechanical, photocopying, recording or otherwise (except under the statutory exceptions provisions of the Australian Copyright Act 1968) without the prior written permission of the publisher.

Irene Emily Louise Mutton
nee Morris

1920 – 1988

[signature: I. Mutton]

PETER JAMES BOND, PUBLISHER
PO BOX 964, ROSNY PARK 7018, TASMANIA, AUSTRALIA

Irene Emily Louise Mutton (nee Morris)

Irene Emily Louise Mutton (nee Morris)

CONTENTS

Introduction 6
Irene Emily Louise Morris 7
The War Years and Aftermath 9
Memories 18
Extracts from *The Spice of Life* 21

Opposite.
Rene on her wedding day, 3 February 1945.

Irene Emily Louise Mutton (nee Morris)

Introduction

This slim volume was created as a tribute to our late mother, who would have turned 100 this year, 2020. With modern advancements in health care, many people are now able to reach this age milestone. Unfortunately for Mum, she was unable to benefit from such advancements and passed away shortly before her 68th birthday. At one time this was considered to have been a 'good innings' but no age is a big enough number to lose your mother. We were, respectively, 33 and (almost) 27 years old. That's old enough to understand but young enough to have felt cheated on her behalf.

Our father self-published his memoirs, *The Spice of Life*, in 2002, as a multi-ring bound book. This volume was republished in trade paperback 10 years later. Both editions were well received by relatives and friends. Of course, Mum features prominently in the content, though her memoirs were never recorded. This is a regret of many people who suffer a family loss. While it can never be rectified, the publication you now hold goes some way to remedying the situation in our case.

We hope that in some small measure it fills a void for those who knew Rene.

- Peter Bond
- Graham Himmelhoch-Mutton

◆

Irene Emily Louise Morris

Irene Emily Louise was born to Arthur and Florence Morris on 8 October 1920. Her birth certificate details the family address as 1 Avon Place, Swan Street, Southwark, Newington North, County of London. An 1896 Ordnance Survey map shows Avon Place as Swan Place.

Southwark is the oldest part of South London and dates back to Roman times, though evidence of prehistoric activity has been unearthed by archaeologists. Fast forward through Anglo-Saxon, medieval and post-medieval times to 1920 and Southwark is an urbanised area. Today, small residences such as 1 Avon Place have given way to multi-storey buildings of residential and commercial function. Ordnance Survey maps of 1936 and 2014, clearly illustrate the development of intervening years.

The earliest photo we have is one of her standing on the steps of (we presume) the family home in Avon Place. She would certainly recognise very little of her birthplace in 2020. Avon Place today is

c1930 Four of the Morris children. Rene, aged about 9 (the youngest), at bottom right.

a utilitarian thoroughfare with little indication of its older-style residential past.

1920 was a vastly different time compared to 2020. Despite being only five generations distant, everyday life then would appear primitive to a youngster today. Arthur and Florence Morris, born in the 1880s, may have thought they were raising their family in a thoroughly modern century. Transport and communications, for example, were more efficient than they had been just a few decades before. On the other hand, living conditions provided by low incomes meant raising a family was always a struggle. Social welfare, as we enjoy it today, was not yet known.

Rene, as she became universally known, was the youngest of five. Her siblings were Ernest (born 1910), Florence (1913), Arthur (1915) and Doris (1917). We know little of the Morris family's life in those early years. Of her childhood, Rene spoke hardly at all. We do know that she and her youngest brother Ernest were considered the clever ones of the family. Rene was educated at the Charles Dickens School in London where girls of under-privileged families showing above-average literary skills were awarded scholarships which gave higher educational opportunities. She later recorded that Dickens' *Bleak House* was her favourite of his novels.

In later life, when retired and living at Bridgewater, she worked tirelessly for the under-privileged of that community, notably deserted wives, widows and single mothers. She would tell them 'I was born in a London slum, I know what it's like to live in poverty.' As a vigorous advocate for the improvement of conditions for her charges, she became chair of the management committee of Neighbourhood House[1].

◆

---

1 Neighbourhood Houses are organisations offering programs which respond to community needs and provide access to community and service systems.

Irene Emily Louise Mutton (nee Morris)

The War Years and Aftermath

We know extraordinarily little about Mum's early years. What life must have been like growing up in 1920s inner London we can only guess because she never spoke of her childhood, and very rarely of her experiences during World War 2, and even less of the immediate years after.

It was not until after her death in 1988 that we began to understand how difficult her life in Britain had been and why she refused to ever speak of it.

Life would have been tough enough in the 1920s and 1930s, but the outbreak of war would have been an inevitable horror that no-one wanted to see. The intensity of it, especially those early years could not have been foreseen. The Blitz, those intense and frequent German bombing raids over London and surrounding areas during 1940 and 1941 must have been hell to live through,

1940s Eric and Rene.

9

Irene Emily Louise Mutton (nee Morris)

and of the very, very few times Mum ever talked of the war it was to say, in as few words as possible, that we as youngsters in peaceful, affable Australia could not even *begin* to imagine the horror of those times. In those moments of recollection, Mum would stare off into space for a few moments, then abruptly change the subject or return her attention to her crocheting or cooking or whatever it was she was doing before she had been so rudely interrupted with talk of those earlier years.

. WRNS recruiting poster.

What was clear to us back then was that she did not want to be reminded of those times, and even less be asked to speak of them, and so we simply did not. Dad, especially, never dared raise the subject. It was only many years later that he began to reveal what had happened in those horrendous years between the start of the Second World War and their departure for Australia in 1958.

Mum was still just 17 at the outbreak of war in September 1939. She joined the Women's Royal Naval Service in June of 1942, a fateful decision which, in the course of her duties as a grade 'A' Air Mechanic, led to her meeting Dad. What is not on record and wasn't widely known until well after her death were some of the other duties she performed during her service in London. It wasn't until the mid-1990s, half a century after the actual events, when reminiscing about the war years, Dad revealed that as a very young woman during the Blitz, while most people were taking cover in the air raid shelters that had become the nightly habitat for all Londoners, our mother

Irene Emily Louise Mutton (nee Morris)

was keeping watch on one of the numerous bridges that spanned the Thames and which were a prime target for German bombers. Her task, whilst enduring the literal bombardment of Nazi high explosives was to stand there, as bombs exploded all around, any one of which could have snuffed out her life in an instant, and plot and record in the pitch dark the location of any mines dropped into the river by the Germans and any bombs which fell close by but failed to explode. As roughly 10% of German bombs at that time failed to detonate, there would have been quite a number to record for the UXB teams to find and defuse once the raid was over. I failed then, and fail still, to understand how she could have performed such duty knowing that at any moment her life, which had barely begun, could be taken from her with the only notice being the shrill, descending whine of a bomb closing in on her location. 'Nerves of steel' don't even begin to describe the courage required, and when our father explained all this to us so many years later, it was in hushed tones of almost indescribable deep respect and awe for the unbelievable bravery she displayed.

1940s Rene in uniform.

Irene Emily Louise Mutton (nee Morris)

At the start of the war, she was living in Avon Place, close to the Thames and therefore in real danger from the overhead bombers targeting the bridge crossings. According to the National Archives bomb census, her home took close to a direct hit, but if it caused her to move house she moved only closer to danger, her address at the time of her release from the WRNS at war's end being Friar's Close, Bear Lane, closer again to the Thames and which itself had several near misses.

Survive though, she did. Excelling at her role in the WRNS as an air mechanic led to her meeting Dad when they were both posted to *RNAS Lee-on-Solent,* very close to Dad's home in Gosport, Hampshire. Assigned to work together Mum immediately impressed our father by drawing out the entire hydraulic system of the Spitfire from memory.

Their work together blossomed into romance and they were married in February 1945. The end of the war in September of that year brought a period of relief to the young couple, but with post-war rationing and Dad's frequent absences during his

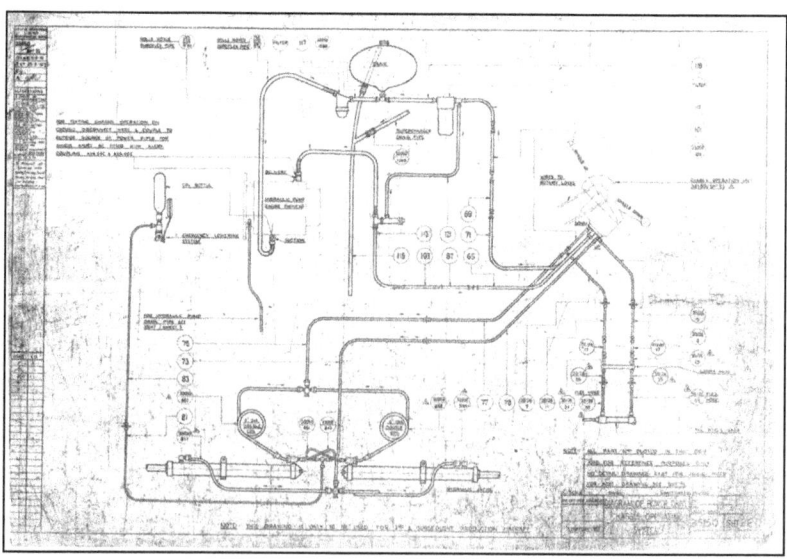

The hydraulic systm of the Supermarine Spitfire, which Rene could draw from memory.

Irene Emily Louise Mutton (nee Morris)

service with the Merchant Navy, life was still tough. 'Many's the time we struggled to find tuppence for a loaf of bread' was one of the very few references I remember Mum making about just how difficult those times were.

The arrival of their first child, Bob, in 1947 and their second, Denis, in 1949 doubtless brought joy, but with them further struggles, but those were soon to be compounded. In 1950 Mum's father died, followed just a year later by the loss of Denis at just two years of age to toxaemia and acute gastroenteritis. With Dad away at sea at the time, it was an especially bitter blow from which she never fully recovered, in her grief giving away or destroying everything connected with Denis. It wasn't until well into my teenage years that I even learnt of Denis' existence, such was her determination to blot the grief from her memory.

Yet even more grief and more troubles were soon to follow even this immense tragedy. Rene's Mum died the following year, 1952, and then in 1953 the Great Flood saw them lose their home in Dovercourt, Essex, as well as nearly all their possessions. Standing on the upper floor of their flooded house, their next-door neighbour already drowned in his cellar, and with their possessions floating around in filthy seawater and sewage downstairs, it must have seemed as if everything imaginable had turned against them.

The birth of their third son Peter in 1955 and a resurgence of interest in the local football team provided some respite, but the lure of a life overseas in warm, sunny Australia had made a strong call on them both. So it was they packed everything and left the old country for Australia in 1958, two young sons in tow, a modest collection of belongings, and dreams of leaving all that misery behind.

Born three years later in 1961, I grew up blissfully unaware of all the troubles they had seen. Life was largely peaceful through the 1960s, with peace and the simple life being, for obvious reasons, the priority. Bob's marriage and arrival of their first

Irene Emily Louise Mutton (nee Morris)

grandchild, Andrew, in the latter part of the decade brought increasing joy and I remember them as being happy times for all. And compared to her wartime and post-war experiences, life in Australia must have seemed comparative bliss. Even when times became a little trickier after Dad's business venture failed, Mum

1966 Bob and Mary's wedding, 12 November.

simply knuckled down, found a job and got on with it to ensure all the debts were paid. She had known plenty of truly hard times already, and a small matter of a failed business was not going to worry her overmuch.

And so, growing up, Mum made sure we never lacked for anything and I was blissfully unaware of those financial struggles. We were always well-fed, appropriately clothed and housed comfortably. Holidays away were rare, to be sure, but frequent day trips away to family-favourite haunts ensured we never felt deprived. They were happy days, and only much later did we learn of the troubles they had back in England and the reasons for their emigration to Australia.

The one significant blip to this happiness was the death of Bob in 1977. A type 1 diabetic, the disease had dogged him all his life, but his untimely demise at the age of just 30, with a wife and three young sons was, of course, an enormous tragedy. Seeing Mum break down when we received the news via telephone has stayed with me ever since, Dad later confirming he feared she would sink to the depths that had caused so much heartache after Denis's death in 1951.

A previously planned trip to the U.K. for later that year was nearly cancelled but went ahead when her doctor suggested it may help her deal with the grief. Although little was said about the trip, I suspect it helped enormously, and perhaps also prompted the visit to Australia a few years later by her brother Arthur which brought her additional comfort.

Mum died way too young not so many years later when just short of her 68th birthday, the last 30 of those years having lived in Australia. In that time she had made just that one return trip to England, about which she had said very little, but I like to think she made peace with the country that had caused her so much grief in her formative years. She spent her remaining time happily enough working and then retiring to a life of civil service as a councillor and a community services volunteer. Despite

Irene Emily Louise Mutton (nee Morris)

everything she had lived through and suffered, her sense of duty to family and country never wavered. Her final, difficult days as disease took its toll on her body were, as usual, endured without complaint and her final conscious moments were to hold the hand of her baby grandson Stephen (our second child) and smile lovingly at him before slipping into unconsciousness for the last time. After an often dangerous and tumultuous life, she died peacefully in October 1988.

Above and right
1967 Happier times.

Her life was a lesson in perseverance, humility and strength in the face of adversity as well as the importance of showing gratitude for the peaceful times and an appreciation for simplicity along with the ever-present need to help others. That she was able to do this despite everything she lived through is an even bigger lesson to us all.

Had she lived to be 100, she would have refused to have any sort of fuss made of her. Instead then, may this tribute be a small, but appropriate reflection of her life.

- Graham

Irene Emily Louise Mutton (nee Morris)

Memories

Inevitably one has favourite memories. Curiously they aren't necessarily of important or significant events but rather, the minutiae of one's life that makes it unique. These are some of my memories.

- Peter

School

From our Toorak Avenue, Lenah Valley home, Mum would walk me the short distance up the hill to preschool. I would always wistfully watch her leave and shout 'Mum, what's the time?' just before she passed out of view. In my filing cabinet is every school report I ever received, starting with grade 1a at Princes Street Primary School. For the first few years a parent needed to sign those reports, thus I have Mum's signature as a memento. I attended Princes Street from grades 1 to 4, but by 1965 we had moved north to Springfield Avenue, West Moonah. It fell to Mum to enrol me at Moonah Primary. When that enrolment was messed up, and phone calls couldn't resolve it, Mum marched down to the school – it was about 10-minutes' walk – and 'sorted them out.' That was Mum, things had to be done, and done right.

1963

When our parents 'had the shop' – on the corner of Hampden Road and Runnymede Street, Battery Point – the shopkeeper role fell mostly to Mum, as Dad worked full-time in his shipwright surveyor job with the Marine Board. Not quite open-all-hours, the hours were nevertheless long and Mum also had her household chores to deal with, cooking, cleaning and looking after her three sons until Dad came home. I enjoyed the benefit of a regular treat from the shop, with Mum's blessing, usually chocolate-based items such as a Tosca, Crispin or Wagon Wheel. I suspect my wise mother knew that I would eventually tire of such luxuries, which I did. It wasn't a daily routine. She would also save the bottle tops of Cascade cordials that youngsters had bought to-drink-here[2]. Removing the cork seal of these bottle tops revealed the face of a TFL footballer. Thanks to Mum I had the complete set in a very short time.

1971

My last year at Cosgrove High School. One day I arrived home from school and told Mum I'd seen a presentation about 'the school trip' which was for B-class (year 10) students, later in the year. It was a two-week trip to Sydney, then as far north as Cairns, returning via Melbourne. I was only vaguely interested but Mum must have sensed something deeper and asked if I wanted to go. She offered to pay for it, so long as I saved my spending money. I think it was going to cost $200 – which sounds very cheap now – but we had some months to save. Mum was working at Silk & Textiles at the time, trying to support Dad's struggling business on Main Road, Glenorchy. That she would do this for me at a difficult time was typical Mum, eager to help others, particularly of course her sons. Or maybe it was just me, was I her favourite?

1975

I flew the nest, actually a comfortable brick and tile three-bedroom house at Bridgewater, and took a flat 'in town.' It was a crummy bed-sit in Sandy Bay, costing $20 a week. Dad helped me move and Mum provided me with (almost) a kitchen full of utensils, crockery and cutlery, and offered one piece of advice, 'Always have biscuits on hand for your guests.' Again, she was thinking of others. Mum and Dad visited me just once after I'd settled in, and Mum immediately took over the tiny kitchen washing up the

---

2 Soft drinks were sometimes consumed in shops with the bottle returned to shopkeepers. Takeaways were a penny dearer.

dishes from the previous day, or perhaps a couple of previous days. The flat came with an ancient washing machine which was never going to work. Of course, every Saturday I took a bag load of laundry 'home' to Bridgewater where Mum would wash, dry and iron my clobber. In 1975 I relied on busses for transport, so this was not entirely convenient. My purchase of a second-hand twin tub washing machine enabled me to stop that ritual and save my suffering mother time and effort. I think she missed my weekly visits but I encouraged the bus drivers of the day by taking the nearly empty bus to Bridgewater once a fortnight.

Mum was an avid reader. She loved detective novels and always had a few on hand borrowed from the library. I like to think it was from her that I gained my love of reading. She wasn't a great buyer of books. That was too illogical. I, on the other hand, buy far too many books, but I think she'd sort of understand. I'd certainly get a mocking 'Well, I'm sure you're right' if I attempted to justify it. That was her way of saying I was completely wrong but she couldn't be bothered arguing the point.

◆

Irene Emily Louise Mutton (nee Morris)

Extracts from *The Spice of Life*

The Spice of Life is our father's autobiography, published in 2002 and again in 2012. It was preceded by a lengthy oral history recorded by Graham in 1994. Covering his war service, post-war life and immigration to Tasmania, it was this recording which prompted Eric to write about his life. Following are extracts from *The Spice of Life* and of the recordings which didn't make it into his published memoirs.

Second World War and Marriage

'The shortage of skilled mechanics had become a problem, relieved by WRNS[3] mechanics coming from the technical training schools. Very capable young ladies, they were well trained in theory, but short on practical work. With the amount of work on hand, we were soon able to give them the experience they needed.

'One of them, Wren Irene Morris, was assigned to me to learn the ropes. She had passed out from training, top of her class with a 90% pass rate. She could draw the complete hydraulic system of a Spitfire from memory and understood the theory of flight better than I. Wren Morris was assigned to the FAA as a trainee air mechanic because of her peacetime occupation as a machinist. Notwithstanding the fact that the only machine she had used was a sewing machine, she was deemed to be suitable for training as a mechanic.

'As already mentioned, after training she was drafted to *RNAS Lee-on-Solent* where she was directed to work with me. What aroused my interest in her, I think, was the fact that she was older and more mature than most of her companions, had already served nearly two years on active service, and was a very capable person. We got along well together, on duty as well as socially and a romance slowly developed.

---

3   The Women's Royal Naval Service (WRNS) was the women's branch of the Royal Navy. Its members were popularly and officially known as Wrens.

Irene Emily Louise Mutton (nee Morris)

1945   Rene and Eric were married in uniform, 3 February.

Irene Emily Louise Mutton (nee Morris)

'On the first day I put a drill through her hand – it just drew blood a little bit – and the next day while we were riveting I hit her finger with a hammer. And we never looked back. She said "I better marry this fellow before he does any more harm".

'My parents took to her straight away, as her family accepted me when she took me to London to meet them. Her father was an ex-navy man who had served in the 1914-18 war so we got along famously. I don't recall ever proposing to her, we both, I suppose, taking it for granted that we would eventually marry, which we did early in 1945.'

'The (D-Day) invasion was 6 June 1944, and we were together from February. We didn't have a clue what was going on. We weren't married then, but Rene used to come home to my parent's place and spend the weekends there. We went back to base one Monday morning and it was just one mass of aircraft flying in and out. We went straight into our overalls and to work.'

'As I said, work was fairly routine and I was fortunate in being able to go on weekend leave frequently. I used to enjoy travelling to London with Rene for shows and to see the sights. It was the time of the V2 rockets, a bit scary as there was never any warning, just a gigantic explosion, sometimes quite close. Surprisingly, like the V1, as a terror weapon, it was a failure, people were fatalistic about it and didn't worry too much.

'Our courtship was proceeding smoothly, Rene spending all her off duty time with me, mostly at home with my parents. Keen cyclists, we would often explore the surrounding countryside. Not only enjoying the balmy spring weather but with so much activity preceding the forthcoming invasion of Europe, there was always something of interest to observe. Sometimes we were lucky in finding a country inn where we could enjoy a quiet drink and if we were very lucky, have a meal too.

Irene Emily Louise Mutton (nee Morris)

'On one such outing, we had cycled to Hillhead, a quiet seaside village that I had visited on several occasions before the war. This time it was a scene of feverish activity, on the foreshore were huge concrete structures that appeared to have no particular purpose. Curious, we stopped to look but were immediately confronted by two Redcaps (Military Police) who demanded our identity books and asked the reason for our presence in the area. Finally satisfied, they let us go, ordering us to leave the area and do our courting elsewhere.'

'Within three years (of leaving the navy) I was back at sea because I got so restless working alongside the water seeing navy ships coming in and going out and Rene finally said, "Well, if you want to go you'd better go, you're no good moping around like this", so I got a job on a salvage ship as a ship's carpenter.'

1951

'... my first winter aboard *Patricia* passed quickly. I was able to spend frequent weekends at home in Gosport. Rene found that being the wife of a sailor could be a lonely existence, especially in a small town. But with a small circle of friends and trips to London to visit her parents, she didn't complain about my absence. Sometimes I would travel down to London from Harwich, staying with her parents and spend happy weekends with her and the boys.'

'One foggy night whilst we were anchored at the tiny port of St. Mary's in the Scilly Isles, tragedy struck. We received a radio message that my son Denis was seriously ill and I was needed at home urgently. The RAF was willing to fly me to Portsmouth, but unfortunately, dense fog precluded any flying, or even for a boat to take me off the island so that I could catch a train from Penzance.

'The fog lifted slightly at dawn and I was able to persuade the ferry skipper to make an early start so that I would be in time to catch the first train to London. It was a long, long journey, made even longer when on reaching London, I phoned the hospital in Portsmouth, only to be told that Denis had died. The two hours ride to Portsmouth, then the ferry and bus ride to home was sheer misery. As you may guess, when I arrived home Rene was in a terrible state and being cared for by a neighbour.

'I can't describe the torment to a young mother when a two-year-old infant dies suddenly, as Denis did. He had suffered what was then described as severe gastroenteritis, dying within a few hours of being admitted to hospital. It also happened that a number of children in Portsmouth and Gosport had been infected that weekend, seven of them proving fatal. The cause was never discovered. The surgeon could only say that in each case, it was the worst ulceration of the bowel he had ever seen.

'After the funeral – Denis was cremated at Southampton – Rene had a nervous breakdown, she didn't cry until three weeks

1966 Graham, Rene and Eric enjoying sunshine in the garden at Springfield Avenue, West Moonah.

Irene Emily Louise Mutton (nee Morris)

1972
Graham, Rene and friend Bertha at Mt. Field National Park.

1972
Rene at Wyndham Road, Claremont.

1973
Friends Una and Sid Wright with Eric and Rene at Baskerville Raceway.

later. She was very ill, behaving in a manner I found to be very distressing. She gave away or destroyed everything in any way connected with Denis, clothes, toys, cot, even photographs. The latter, to this day I find saddening as I have no recollection of what he looked like all those years ago.

'Rene blamed herself for his death and me for being away at sea. Her doctor advised that perhaps a change of environment might help. Rene agreed, so we sold our home and moved to Harwich where we wouldn't be separated so frequently.'

1952 - Olympic Games

'After two interest-filled weeks in Helsinki... my homecoming wasn't the joyous reception that I had expected. Rene was still suffering from acute depression following Denis' death and my prolonged absence from home only made things worse.

'I was faced with a decision... I reluctantly tendered my resignation from Trinity House and paid off from *THV Patricia*. That decision was another watershed in my life and a wise one. I still had my work with ships and quickly settled down to shore life.

'It was worth it to see Rene's improvement in health. It took time to recover from Denis' death but being together helped us both. Yes, I had been selfish, had had an interesting and exciting time but was happy to be settling down to family life.'

1953 - North Sea Flood

'In February 1953, weather conditions were bad, with gale-force winds blowing for days on end bringing extremely cold conditions from the Arctic Ocean. These winds, coupled with the spring tides drove the waters of the North Sea southwards so that low-lying areas of East Anglia and Holland were inundated by abnormally high tides.

'Our house was at the lower end of the street, below the level of the sea wall. This sea wall was an embankment on top of

Irene Emily Louise Mutton (nee Morris)

1973
Christmas in Sydney with the Fitzgerald family.

1973
In the garden at Wyndham Road, Claremont.

1973
Rene and Graham at Claremont with one of the family's many cats.

Irene Emily Louise Mutton (nee Morris)

which were the railway lines serving the train ferry depot in the old part of Harwich. In the early hours of a Sunday morning, we were awakened by frantic knocking on our front door. It was a neighbour bringing the news that the sea was spilling over the top of the sea wall and flooding was imminent.

'Rene and I rushed downstairs to the basement to move as much as we could of our food and belongings up to the first floor. My last task was to get buckets of coal for our upstairs fireplace. I was just filling my third bucket when the seawall was breached. The back door burst in and icy cold seawater flooded into the basement.

'... at number 17, Rene and I stood shivering at the top of the stairs viewing with dismay our treasured possessions floating around in that filthy water. There was not much we could do but at least we could keep warm upstairs and have something to eat. Young Bob, just turned six, thought it a great adventure. My main concern was for him and Rene. Obviously, it was best that they go to stay with her family in London.

'I sent Rene to London with Bob and she had quite a job just getting there. First of all she had to get to about 20 miles away which was as far as the train could go – they took her up in a truck I think, with a lot of other women and children being taken away. I stayed there in Harwich and she went up to her mother in London and stayed there until we got the water out of the place.

'Three weeks after the flood and after a lot of hard work, the house was warm and dry enough for me to go to London to collect Rene and Bob. But it took a long time to restore our home to any semblance of comfort.'

1955

'For a time, both Rene and I were keen fans of our local football (soccer) team and enjoyed travelling with them to their away games around Essex and Suffolk. Came the time when we had to curtail all that activity, we were 'infanticipating'. Our son Peter was born at home, 17 Victoria Street, on the longest day of the year, 21 June 1955. The period was known as the Post-War Baby Boom, a busy time for hospitals and maternity homes.

'To cope with the great demand for beds, the Health Department encouraged mothers to have their babies at home, supplying all the necessities and midwifery services for the event. Rene had a trouble-free pregnancy so we agreed to a home birth. A few days before B-Day, we took delivery of a large carton containing all that could possibly be needed for the great day. Being a considerate lady, Rene waited until after breakfast before sending me to fetch the midwife. Then for the next few hours, I was 'bossed' by a large lady who didn't appear to like young fathers cluttering up her workplace.'

1958 – Emigration.

'It was the time when we were being bombarded with advertisements. 'Migrate to Australia,' the ad's said, '£10 ($20) a head, children free.' Surprise surprise, when I broached the subject,

1973
Rene and Graham (with Peter in shadow in the background) visiting the Hawksbury River, Sydney.

never thinking that Rene would agree, she was enthusiastic. We sent in our application, were interviewed at Australia House in London and accepted. I quickly found a job in Townsville where I was to run tourist boats to the Barrier Reef and be responsible for their maintenance.

'Accommodation was to be made available. Sounded great, but unfortunately, Rene's doctor who had been in Townsville during the war advised against it, saying that she would never stand the heat. So we then checked the weather reports for the whole of Australia, finally deciding on Tasmania. I wrote to the secretary of the Royal Hobart Yacht Club who quickly found me a job and agreed to sponsor me. All we had to do then was wait for a ship.

'Sailing from Southampton on a fine, sunny summer evening, Rene and I stood on deck, seeing, perhaps for the last time, the familiar sights of Hampshire, of our former home town Gosport, the oh so familiar entrance to Portsmouth Harbour. To starboard, my favourite prewar playground, the Isle of Wight. It brought a lump to my throat. 'What have we let ourselves in for?' I said. No reply. I guess she felt as I did.

'Rene was seasick and took to her bunk, there she stayed, right through Biscay and the Mediterranean until we docked at Port Said. The skills of our steward, even the ships doctor's attentions were to no avail.

'After a few hours ashore (at Aden) we continued through the Red Sea. Once into the Indian Ocean, again we struck bad weather, once more, Rene taking to her bunk. There she stayed until we reached Fremantle.

'I digress a while here to explain that as far as seasickness goes, Rene was incurable. I have known her to be violently ill even on a cruise from Hobart up-river to New Norfolk.'

1963 - The Shop

'As my job necessitated a lot of travelling around Tasmania, I was away from home quite a lot. To keep herself occupied, Rene

Irene Emily Louise Mutton (nee Morris)

Above
1974
Friend Una Wright and Rene.

Right
1976
Caught by surprise in the kitchen at Finlay Street, Bridgewater.

Below
1975
A family portrait –
Graham, Bob and Peter.
Rene and Eric.
In the living room at Finlay Street, Bridgewater.

found part-time work helping in a small shop, a typical corner store which sold just about everything, groceries, confectionery, cigarettes. Unknown to us at the time, it was going to make great changes to our lives. The premises had been owned by an elderly lady who had traded there for many years. On her retirement she sold the business, retaining the premises, which she leased to the new owners.

'They were a young couple having a difficult time, or at least the wife was. She was trying to manage the shop, care for two children and run the home whilst her ne'er-do-well husband spent most of his time gambling and drinking at one of Hobart's less reputable hotels, financed by helping himself to the contents of the shop's till.

'With no previous experience in business, she was fighting a losing battle. Rene helped her for a few hours each day but it was obvious that the losses were becoming astronomical. Finally, the poor woman had had enough. She just walked out, abandoning the shop, and with her two children caught the next flight back to her home in the USA. Her husband took off after her the following day.

'The owner of the property called on Rene to tell her the news and offered her the business, immediate start and for only the price of the stock. So, for the princely sum of £300 ($600), we were in business. I still retained my Marine Board job so we could afford to engage part-time help for the shop. Even so, it was very hard work. I would get home after work, have a quick tea then help in the shop. We were open seven days a week, closing at 8 or 9 pm. On Saturdays, I would do the rounds of the wholesalers buying stock.'

1969 - Eric Mutton Marine Surveys

'That first year looked promising, business was good and I was able to build up my stock to a presentable level. At the same time I was getting survey work, insurance claims assessing and valuations for finance companies. Not enough to keep me going full time but useful sidelines nonetheless. My problem was that being a one-man operation, I had to frequently shut shop for a day to do those jobs. Rene helped as best she could, but knowing little about the boating industry and with young boys to raise she wasn't always in a position to take over whilst I was away.

She surprised me one day however when returning from a yacht survey, I found her in the shop with four men teaching them how to splice an eye in a length of rope. She could do a far neater splice than I, learning the art during her spell in the navy. Another feature of her skills was to be able to make boat covers from reinforced plastic sheeting, complete with spliced rope ties. As a sideline too, she made waterproof coats for greyhounds, many of which were exercised in the district.'

1976 Rene, Eric's sister Wyn and her husband Reg, in the garden at Finlay Street, Bridgewater.

Irene Emily Louise Mutton (nee Morris)

1972

'Came the time when my bank balance was so deeply in the red that I had to admit defeat. Some thousands of dollars in debt, I was obliged to shut up shop and put myself at the mercy of my creditors. They were in the main, very good about it. To avoid bankruptcy I had arranged to repay an agreed sum monthly to their appointed agent. That I managed to do well within the estimated time.

1976   Rene, Eric, Wyn and Reg in the Fuscia House, Royal Tasmanian Botanical Gardens, Hobart.

'It was, however, a traumatic time for me. Although Rene wasn't wholly in favour of my business venture at the outset, all she said was, 'Don't worry about it, I'll get myself a job,' which was what she wanted to do in the first place. I was extremely worried, with the result that one day I had a blackout. My doctor, on hearing my story diagnosed acute depression, advising that I get out my toolkit, put on a pair of overalls and go back to where I started, doing what I knew I could do well. I took his advice.

'Meanwhile Rene had started work as a machinist with a leading textile company (Silk and Textiles), quickly rising to a responsible position, which in turn resulted in her being offered a better position with a newly established soft furnishing company (Moonah Décor) at a very attractive salary.'

1977 - Bob's death

'… tragedy again struck. Whilst picnicing with Mary and baby Cameron, then just a year old, Bob went canoeing at Sydney's Lane Cove, got into difficulties and was drowned. The coroner's

1977
Rene and Eric relaxing at Christmas, Bridgewater.

verdict was accidental drowning but I believe that as a result of his extra exertions, he suffered a diabetic hypo, went into a coma and his canoe capsized.

'It was a terrible shock to us both, particularly to Rene who showed all the symptoms of her previous illness after the death of Denis. The subsequent funeral in Sydney was an ordeal for us both, but in Rene's case it left lasting consequences.'

1977 – Holiday to UK

'Some months previously we had planned a holiday in the UK but were of a mind to cancel it. Rene's doctor advised against cancellation, saying that an overseas holiday would be the best treatment for her state of mind. Family and friends were of the same opinion and persuaded us to go ahead with our plans. So in September 1977, leaving Peter and Graham, then very capable young men, to fend for themselves we left Melbourne on a Qantas flight to London via Singapore and Bahrain.

'Our itinerary consisted solely of visits to our families and friends. Grieving as we were, we were not in a 'holiday mood', not geared to going to exciting places of interest. To be with our families would be sufficient to take us out of our despondency, and that is precisely what happened. I could see a change in Rene when she was with her sisters. I too was feeling better for the happy atmosphere of our reunions. True, there were emotional moments with those that we had farewelled nearly 20 years before, but they were also joyful occasions.

'London being our starting point, we were met by Rene's niece June and her husband Henry who took us to their home in Orpington, Kent, which being within easy reach of London, was to be our base for the first part of our stay. It was a delightful start to our holiday, all Rene's brothers and sisters lived fairly close to each other in south-east London, making a grand family reunion easy to arrange. Her elder brother Arthur and his wife Eva were then our hosts for a few days. We were able to return their hospitality the following year when they came to Tasmania to spend a month with us.

'Another long time friend is Pam, who served with Rene in the WRNS during the war and was matron of honour at our wedding. With her and her husband, we spent a lovely day at their home in Hertfordshire.'

1980s – Retirement

'Rene and I had both developed interests in community work, I volunteering for work with the Arthritis Foundation, Rene preferred working with children, choosing the local primary and high schools for voluntary activities.

'In 1984 I became ill with a severe attack of shingles… Rene wasn't enjoying the best of health and having to care for me didn't improve matters. What worried us most was the fact that our son

1977 Rene with her sister Flo in London.

Irene Emily Louise Mutton (nee Morris)

Graham was to be married in Sydney in September and we both wanted to be there.'

'... some four years later Rene herself was very ill. In 1985 Rene's illness was beginning to cause some concern and necessitated my spending more time with her. Although she had been ailing for some time Rene had been busying herself with the local high school, the primary school and Neighbourhood House, the latter, a drop-in centre for disadvantaged women, where she had been appointed chairperson of the management committee. She had been asked to get together a small group of elderly people to work with the grade 10 high school students in the speech and drama class.

'I was one of the five she had persuaded to take part. Much to my surprise, it was an extremely interesting experience. At our first meeting, the students asked us to tell them of our lives when we were young. What interested them most was the story of how Rene and I met during the war. They were so intrigued that with the help of their class teacher, they wrote a play based on our story.

1984   Rene mingling at Graham and Jane's wedding.

'By that time she was very weak and confined to a wheelchair when going out, but that didn't prevent her from attending rehearsals and encouraging the performers, coaching them into memorising their parts. There were 15 students and four of us senior citizens in the cast. I was cast in the role of Great Uncle Claude, an elderly uncle visiting his niece's family in Australia and telling the story of how he met his wife in wartime England. Just as Rene and I had done.'

1988

'... Rene was very ill but was able to attend in her wheelchair. Soon after that, my whole time was taken up with caring for her. We had a 'home help' coming in regularly, which eased the burden for me. Our neighbour, Nellie Jean, the lady who I had taught to swim, popped in from time to time to help out. Not totally confined to her bed, Rene was able to walk about the house,

1985
Eric, Rene and Peter at Finlay Street, Bridgewater.

supervising my attempts at housekeeping, cooking, doing the washing, even showing me the best way of hanging it out to dry.

'I remember her at the stove with a saucepan in her hand saying 'This is a roux, it is used for ... remember, you will soon be doing all this for yourself, so pay attention mate.' She always called me mate when she was in a happy frame of mind.

'She loved her television, particularly the sporting programmes. She was able to see the 1988 Olympic Games from start to finish. Her constant companion was her cat Ferrari, so named because of his loud purr. For entertainment, we would play scrabble and do the crosswords together. We were both good at cryptic crosswords so preferred the more difficult ones like the Times crossword to be found each week in the Weekend Australian.

'She loved to hear me play the old tunes of the twenties and thirties on my organ, sometimes singing to my accompaniment. One such day, she stopped singing and when I looked round, I saw tears streaming down her face. I had been playing Mendelssohn's On Wings of Song which, she later told me, she used to sing with her school choir.

1985   Rene, Eric, Jane and Christopher.

'Then there was her crocheting. I had adapted her set of crochet hooks to suit her badly deformed fingers. She continued to turn out most beautiful work, most of which she promptly gave away.

'Then occurred what I had experienced four years previously. For some time, it had been her wish to revisit once more our family in Brisbane, my nephew Kevin, his wife Val and their two daughters Karen and Belinda, who had been so kind to us on previous visits. Her doctor told her that when she was well enough to travel, she could have her wish. So determined was she that she willed herself to get better, showing signs of improvement in her general condition and in her mental attitude. She was more alert, eager to make plans for her holiday.

'Eventually her doctor felt that the proposed holiday could go ahead. He briefed me on our travel plans. Careful and

1987 Rene and Christopher.

comfortable transport to and from airports and above all total care and attention. He was of the opinion that we could not expect a cure, but having that holiday would probably give her a little extra happiness.

'I couldn't have wished for better co-operation from the airline, a wheelchair with experienced attendants, constant attention throughout the flights to and from Brisbane, to which she responded with her cheerful attitude and an almost childlike eagerness. Settled in Kevin's lovely home in Brisbane, the girls took over, tending to her comfort and chatting constantly.

1988 One of the last photos of Rene and Eric together, taken while on holiday in Brisbane. Rene was teaching the finer points of English pork pie making.

Irene Emily Louise Mutton (nee Morris)

'Her favourite seat was in a shady spot by the swimming pool listening to the sound of running water and the birds singing in the trees. The break did me a power of good too, as I was able, nay, ordered to go into the city and relax. The Brisbane Expo was on at the time, so I managed to see some of the exhibits and attractions.

'Our evenings were spent quietly, playing Scrabble, at which she was particularly adept, and chatting. My most vivid memory of that holiday was arriving home one afternoon, to find her in the kitchen showing the girls how to make a genuine English Pork Pie. It turned out perfectly.

'After two weeks into the holiday she said that she wanted to go home, feeling that she should be back in hospital. Even on the flight home, she chatted happily with fellow passengers, telling them what a lovely holiday that she'd had. When crossing Bass Strait she looked down at the Tasmanian coastline, gripped my hand tightly and said, "Thank you for a lovely holiday, but I am glad to be home again."

'On arrival home, she was admitted into hospital. Her friends visited her and to all of them, she said a cheerful goodbye. But she had had enough. She insisted that the surgeon do an exploratory operation to learn the cause of her illness. "'If I don't come out of it," she said, "so be it."

'I was crying when they took her to the theatre, but she gripped my hand and with a smile said, "Don't worry dear, I'll be OK." I think that they were the last words she ever said to me.

'Later, I was told that she had arteriosclerosis of the intestine, her small intestine was already dead and that they could do nothing to save her. She would die within 12 hours. It was a condition in which blood ceased to flow into the intestines, causing death by starvation. I was later told that is was a quite rare condition, very difficult to diagnose. A few hours later, with Peter, Graham, Jane and me at her side, she quietly passed away.

Irene Emily Louise Mutton (nee Morris)

'At her funeral a few days later, the chapel was full to overflowing with family and friends. She was cremated and her ashes scattered into the river at her favourite picnic spot in Mount Field National Park, Tasmania. Only a few days later, her faithful cat pined for her, became ill and had to be put down.'

- Eric

◆

www.ingramcontent.com/pod-product-compliance
Lightning Source LLC
Chambersburg PA
CBHW061703160426
42811CB00090BB/1070